HOW OLD IS A WHALE?

For my father, and his love of nature
LM

For Olive
JH

First US edition 2023
First published by Big Picture Press, an imprint of Bonnier Books UK, 2022

Library of Congress Catalog Card Number 2022908716
ISBN 978-1-5362-2975-2

22 23 24 25 26 27 TLF 10 9 8 7 6 5 4 3 2 1

Printed in Dongguan, Guangdong, China

This book was typeset in Mattina Sera, Ashbury, and Adobe Caslon.
The illustrations were done in colored pencil and edited digitally.

BIG PICTURE PRESS
an imprint of
Candlewick Press
99 Dover Street
Somerville, Massachusetts 02144

www.candlewick.com

HOW OLD IS A WHALE?

ANIMAL LIFE SPANS FROM THE MAYFLY TO THE IMMORTAL JELLYFISH

LILY MURRAY
ILLUSTRATED BY JESSE HODGSON

BPP

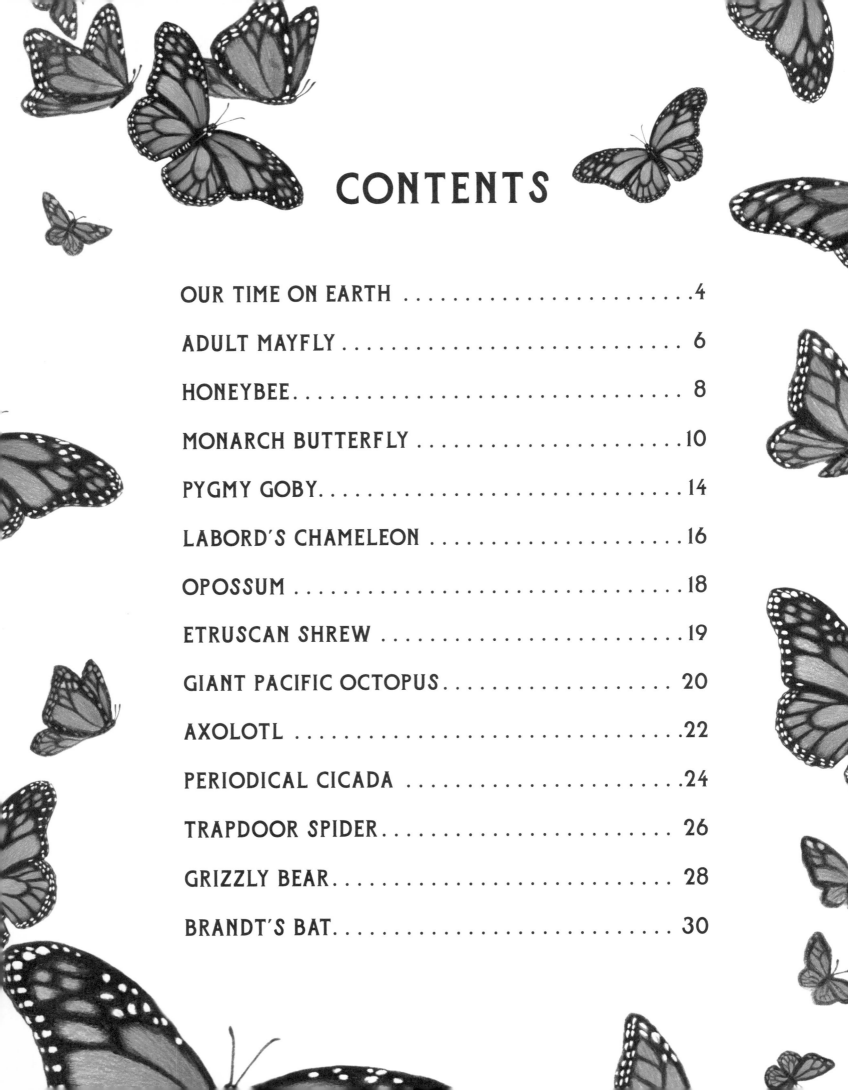

CONTENTS

OUR TIME ON EARTH 4

ADULT MAYFLY 6

HONEYBEE 8

MONARCH BUTTERFLY 10

PYGMY GOBY 14

LABORD'S CHAMELEON 16

OPOSSUM 18

ETRUSCAN SHREW 19

GIANT PACIFIC OCTOPUS 20

AXOLOTL 22

PERIODICAL CICADA 24

TRAPDOOR SPIDER 26

GRIZZLY BEAR 28

BRANDT'S BAT 30

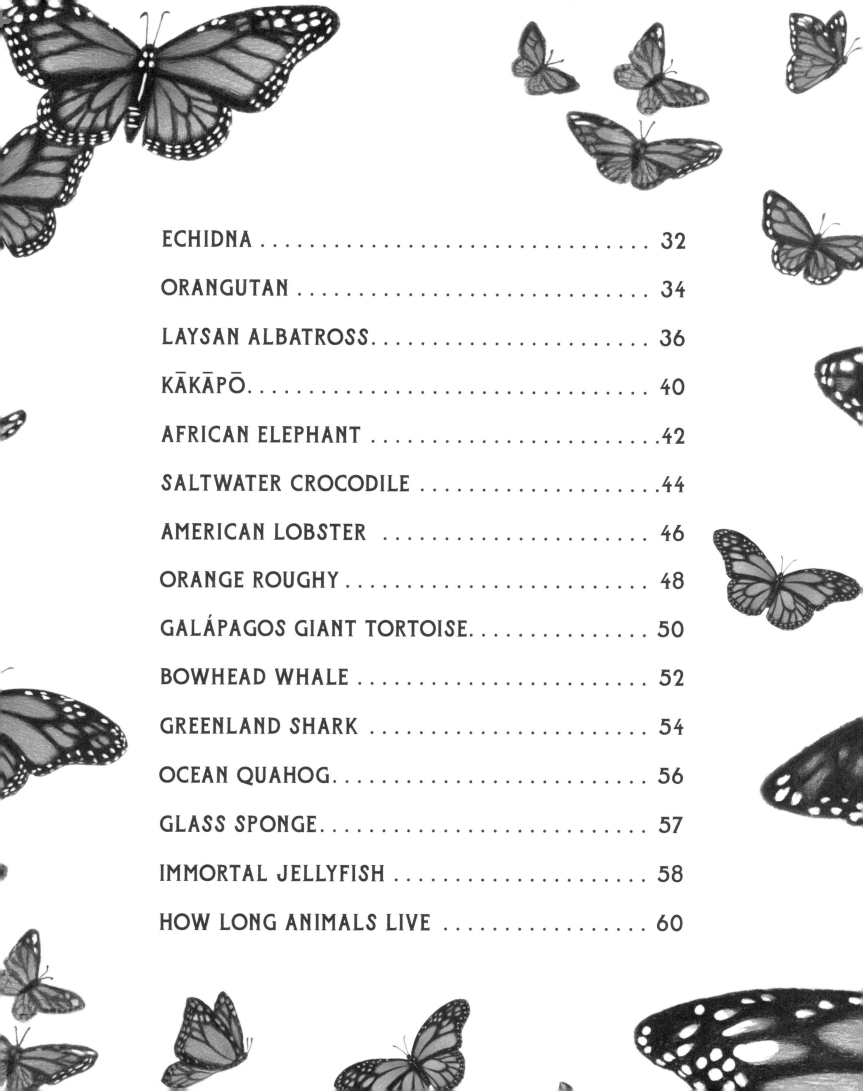

ECHIDNA 32

ORANGUTAN 34

LAYSAN ALBATROSS 36

KĀKĀPŌ 40

AFRICAN ELEPHANT 42

SALTWATER CROCODILE 44

AMERICAN LOBSTER 46

ORANGE ROUGHY 48

GALÁPAGOS GIANT TORTOISE 50

BOWHEAD WHALE 52

GREENLAND SHARK 54

OCEAN QUAHOG 56

GLASS SPONGE 57

IMMORTAL JELLYFISH 58

HOW LONG ANIMALS LIVE 60

OUR TIME ON EARTH

For some creatures, *life* means just a few weeks or months on earth. For others, a lifetime can span hundreds, even thousands, of years. Be it long or short, an animal's allotted life span, encoded within its DNA, dictates so much about the way it lives.

Short-lived animals are in a race against the clock from the moment they are born, needing to mature fast enough to have young of their own before they die. Long-lived animals can take their time and spend their days at a more leisurely pace. Think of a mouse. Its life is usually over within two short years. Meanwhile, a two-year-old elephant is still a baby, suckling milk, never far from its mother's side.

But why is life so short for some and so long for others? Why is it that the Labord's chameleon, in the forests of Madagascar, will never know the dry season? Its five months of existence start and end with the rains. How is it that a giant tortoise can live to a hundred and go for a year without eating, but a Etruscan shrew must frantically find food every two hours to survive?

Does the power of flight bring with it the gift of longer life? And why do so many of the longest-lived creatures inhabit the freezing waters of the deep?

This book seeks the answers to the secrets of longevity. It also reveals how understanding animals' life spans can provide intriguing insights into their existence.

Along the way, you'll meet a fascinating array of creatures, from the gossamer-winged mayfly to the curious axolotl and the majestic albatross.

Read on to discover what these amazing animals make of their time on earth.

ADULT MAYFLY

LIFE SPAN: 5 MINUTES TO 24 HOURS

Fast, fleeting, and fascinating . . . the adult mayfly's life span is one of the shortest in the animal world. From the moment a mayfly emerges in its adult form, it is in a race against time to find a mate and breed.

A mayfly's life begins in the water. For up to two years, a young mayfly lives out its nymph (or larval) stage at the bottom of ponds, lakes, and rivers, feeding on algae and plants. When a nymph reaches its adult stage, it floats to the surface. There, its outer layer splits open and it emerges with wings.

At first, an adult mayfly is dull-colored and seeks shelter in vegetation along the bank. But a few hours later, it sheds its skin one last time and transforms into its final, delicate form, with a shiny body and translucent wings.

The clock is now ticking. Most mayflies have less than twenty-four hours to fulfill their purpose. For one species, *Dolania americana*, there is only a brief five minutes.

The males gather above the water in huge swarms. Females join them in the search for a mate. This is feast time for predators. Birds swoop through the air with open beaks, frogs flick out their sticky tongues, and fish leap from the water.

After mating, the female falls back down to the water, dipping her abdomen below the surface to lay her eggs. When she is spent, she dies in the water, while the males fly to ground nearby to die. The eggs sink to the bottom, where they stick to plants and stones. A few days to a few weeks later (depending on the species), the eggs hatch into tiny nymphs, and the life cycle begins again.

An adult mayfly's life may be short, but mayflies have been on earth for more than 300 million years. Today, they survive only in unpolluted water, where the adults still haze the air with their fleeting dance.

HONEYBEE

LIFE SPAN: 5 TO 7 WEEKS

A worker honeybee born in the spring only lives for five to seven weeks, but not a day of her life is wasted. While it is the role of the queen bee to lay eggs, and the male drone bees to mate with the queen, it is the workers who keep the hive running. Throughout her life, a worker will take on an astonishing number of tasks, changing her roles as she ages.

DAYS 1 TO 3

A worker bee emerges from her cell. She is around $\frac{1}{2}$ inch (15 millimeters) in length. One of her first tasks is to clean out her cell to make sure it is spotless and polished, ready to receive new eggs or to store pollen and nectar.

DAYS 3 TO 16

During the first two weeks of her life, a worker bee may take on the role of a mortuary bee. It is her job to remove any dead bees and larvae that have failed to develop.

A worker bee may also act as a nurse bee, caring for the developing larvae by keeping them clean and feeding them a mixture of honey and pollen known as bee bread. Nurse bees will check on a single larva around 1,300 times a day.

DAYS 7 TO 12

A select few of the workers become the queen's attendants, feeding and grooming the queen. While attending her, they are covered in her scent, known as the queen mandibular pheromone (QMP). The attendants then spread QMP throughout the hive, which ensures all the bees remain loyal to their queen.

DAYS 12 TO 18

By day twelve, young worker bees will become pollen packagers, taking nectar and pollen from foraging bees that are returning to the hive and placing them in cells. The pollen will then be mixed with honey and stored as food for the colony.

During this time, worker bees will also take turns as fanning bees, using their wings to keep the hive cool.

DAYS 12 TO 35

At around twelve days old, a worker bee is able to produce waxy flakes from her abdomen. These are used to build new wax combs in the hive. The wax is also used to cap the cells of pupae (bees at the stage between larvae and full-grown), as well as cells filled with ripened honey.

DAYS 18 TO 21

The last task of a worker bee within the hive is to protect it from intruders. By day twelve, her glands have filled with venom so that she can defend the hive from attack. She stands guard at the hive entrance, checking each bee that returns for its familiar scent.

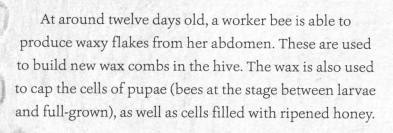

DAYS 22 TO 42

The worker bee is now halfway through her life, and her time outside the hive is about to begin as she takes on the role of forager bee.

As a forager, she will visit up to forty flowers a minute, and may visit more than 1,000 flowers a day. As she flies, she will fill the pollen baskets on her back legs and suck up nectar, storing it in a special honey stomach.

At the end of her time, she will probably die in the field, to be seamlessly replaced by the new worker bees emerging from their cells.

MONARCH BUTTERFLY
LIFE SPAN: 2 WEEKS TO 8 MONTHS

Most monarch butterflies spend their lives on a journey they will never finish. Each year, the butterflies wake from their winter sleep in Mexico and fly north along the coast of North America all the way to Canada. As these butterflies only live for two to six weeks, their journey is one that will take two to three generations to complete. But for the last generation of monarchs, it is a very different story.

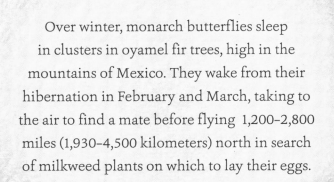

Over winter, monarch butterflies sleep in clusters in oyamel fir trees, high in the mountains of Mexico. They wake from their hibernation in February and March, taking to the air to find a mate before flying 1,200–2,800 miles (1,930–4,500 kilometers) north in search of milkweed plants on which to lay their eggs.

By April, the females have laid their eggs (up to five hundred), dying soon after. The eggs take around four days to hatch into tiny, pale-green, shiny caterpillars. The caterpillars eat their own eggshells before feasting on the leaves of the milkweed plant.

Two weeks later, the caterpillars are fully grown. By now, they are covered in vivid yellow, black, and white stripes. They begin to move farther away from the milkweed plants, then attach themselves to a stem or leaf using silk, and envelop themselves in a chrysalis—a hard, protective outer layer.

It takes just ten days for a monarch butterfly to emerge from its chrysalis. It then flies away, always heading north, feeding on flowers along the way. After five to six weeks, the females lay their eggs, giving way to a new generation of monarchs.

For the next three months, the cycle continues. In May and June, the second generation is usually born, and the third in July and August. Like the monarchs before them, these butterflies will hatch, mate, and fly north, laying their eggs before they die.

September and October sees the hatching of the fourth generation. These monarchs are different from those that have come before. They will live for six to eight months, and in that time they will make an incredible journey of 3,000 miles (4,800 kilometers) all the way back to Mexico.

The monarchs use thermals (patches of warm, rising air) and air currents to help them on their journey, flying by day and roosting together at night in trees. Each morning, they bask in the sun to warm their wings before beginning on their journey once more.

When they reach Mexico, they gather in huge clusters in the oyamel fir trees and sleep till spring.

PYGMY GOBY

LIFE SPAN: 59 DAYS

Among all the beautiful, varied, colorful creatures on a coral reef, the pygmy goby is easy to overlook. It is only $\frac{2}{5}$ inch to $\frac{4}{5}$ inch (1 to 2 centimeters) long, and very well camouflaged in its habitat. But it has recently been discovered to hold an astonishing record—that of the shortest-lived vertebrate, or backboned animal, on the planet. The pygmy goby lives, at most, fifty-nine days. However, it makes up for its brief life by cramming a huge amount of living into a very short span of time.

After hatching, young pygmy goby float out to the open ocean. Three weeks later, they find the nearest coral reef and feast on microscopic prey, such as tiny crustaceans and algae, using the energy from their food to keep growing. At just five weeks old, they are ready to mate. Females lay three clutches of up to four hundred eggs in total, and once their job is done they die shortly after. The final task for males is to fan the eggs with their fins to provide them with a stream of oxygenated water and guard them from predators. The speed of their life cycle is such that seven generations of pygmy goby can be produced in a year.

Scientists think pygmy goby live life at such a fast pace because they have to reach adulthood quickly if they are to stand a chance of mating and having young. Huge numbers of these snack-size fish are gobbled up each day by larger predators on the reef, such as snappers and sea snakes. To keep their population going, the pygmy goby has no choice but to breed fast. And it is their high turnover that makes them hugely important to life on the reef. Without these fish living fast and dying young, a key link in the complex food web of the reef would be lost.

LABORD'S CHAMELEON

LIFE SPAN: 4 TO 5 MONTHS

The Labord's chameleon spends most of its life as an egg. These lizards live in the forests of Madagascar, but for eight months of the year, during the dry season, their eggs slowly incubate in burrows in the sand. When the rains arrive in November, all the eggs hatch at once. The tiny chameleons that emerge have a short, brutal life ahead of them. They have just five months to reach adulthood and breed, making them the shortest-lived (and fastest-growing!) four-legged animals on earth.

After hatching, the tiny chameleons scamper through the branches of the trees, lassoing insects and spiders with their long tongues. They eat so much that they grow at a rate of 2.5 millimeters a day. Many, however, will fall prey to snakes, birds, and monkeys. Those that make it to January are fully grown and ready to mate. The males turn a bright asparagus-green, while the females put on a dazzling display of color to attract mates, turning speckled violet, blue, yellow, and green. After mating, females dig burrows in the sand to lay their eggs, then die, with the males following them to their deaths soon after. At this time, weak, older chameleons can be seen falling from the trees, like dried-up leaves. By April, the forests are once again empty of chameleons. Only their eggs remain, buried in the hot, dry sand.

It seems an extreme life cycle, but it ensures the chameleons are able to survive changes in climate, from the hot, dry season when there is little to eat, to the explosion in insect life that comes with the rains.

OPOSSUM

LIFE SPAN: 1 TO 2 YEARS

Although they grow to be the size of a cat, at birth, a baby opossum is no bigger than a honeybee. A newborn's first act, naked and blind, is to crawl to its mother's pouch, where it must latch on to one of her teats if it is to survive. There, the surviving babies will stay for up to seventy days. As they develop, they spend more and more time outside the pouch, occasionally hitching a ride on their mother's back, before they learn to clamber about by themselves. By just six to eight months, an opossum is fully developed and ready to breed.

Opossums' lives are so short, in part, because there are so many predators around. Opossums that live on islands, where there are fewer predators, have been found to breed later in life. They are able to keep producing litters for longer, and live longer lives.

Interestingly, however, all marsupials have shorter lives for their body size compared to other mammals, and scientists do not yet know why.

ETRUSCAN SHREW

LIFE SPAN: 1 TO 2 YEARS

While opossums are one of the shortest-lived marsupials, shrews are among the shortest-lived mammals. At birth, all mammals (other than humans) have the same lifetime supply of heartbeats: a limit of around one billion. Smaller mammals tend to live shorter lives than larger mammals because their hearts beat more quickly. This is particularly true of the Etruscan shrew, one of the world's smallest mammals, which burns through its heartbeats at a furious rate of up to 1,500 beats per minute.

It is not only the shrew's heart that beats quickly—it does everything in the fast lane. A shrew is constantly on the move, and to keep going, it needs to keep eating, snuffling through the undergrowth in search of insects and spiders. Many shrew species must eat their own body weight in food each day in order to survive. Even a few hours without food can mean death, so shrews never nap for more than a few minutes at a time.

Most shrews won't make it past their first birthday, as they fall prey to owls, snakes, and even trout. But in shrew-time, that's still long enough to have a litter or two of babies and beat out, if not all their allotted billion heartbeats, then something close to it.

GIANT PACIFIC OCTOPUS

LIFE SPAN: 3 TO 5 YEARS

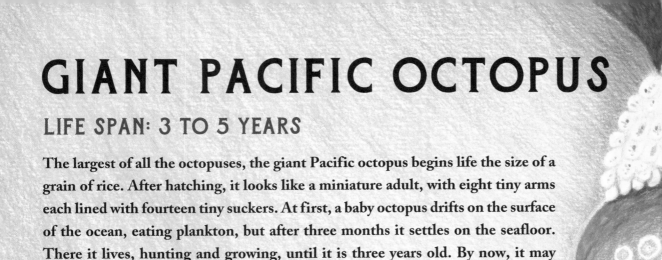

The largest of all the octopuses, the giant Pacific octopus begins life the size of a grain of rice. After hatching, it looks like a miniature adult, with eight tiny arms each lined with fourteen tiny suckers. At first, a baby octopus drifts on the surface of the ocean, eating plankton, but after three months it settles on the seafloor. There it lives, hunting and growing, until it is three years old. By now, it may weigh more than 33 pounds (15 kilograms) with an arm span of up to 16 feet (5 meters). At this point, it is ready to breed.

This, however, is a risky business. Females have a habit of eating males while mating. If they both escape from this encounter alive, the male still dies soon after, while the female heads to a den in deeper water. There, a month later, she lays tens of thousands of tiny eggs, which she weaves together into strands, hanging them from the roof of her den.

The laying of eggs marks the beginning of the end for the female octopus. She will live on for seven more months, watching over her eggs, barely eating and never leaving them. She fans her eggs with her arms or contracts her body and shoots out streams of oxygen-rich water to nourish them. She delicately cleans them with her suckers to keep them clear of algae. Finally, she watches her eggs hatch and her offspring float to the surface. But she will not follow them or parent them, for she is out of time. She has done all she can to help the next generation to survive.

Octopuses are remarkably intelligent. They can solve problems, play tricks, and even mimic one another. Unlike most other intelligent creatures, however, they spend most of their lives alone and their time on earth is short. Why have octopuses evolved to live such brief lives with such amazing intelligence? What is the point of developing such a complex brain if the octopus doesn't have much time to use it?

Perhaps it is because they are so vulnerable to predators. They have no external shells to protect them, but their soft bodies are agile and nimble and can fit into astonishingly small spaces. They rely on their large brains to get them out of trouble—they are able to camouflage themselves in an instant. But even with all this trickery, a soft-skinned octopus cannot expect to survive long in the predator-filled sea. Just as their bodies can squeeze into the smallest of spaces, so they must squeeze the stages of their lives into an all-too-brief life span.

AXOLOTL

LIFE SPAN: 10 TO 15 YEARS

The axolotl is a strange, alien-looking creature found only in the lakes and canals near Mexico City. A species of tiger salamander, it spends its life skulking through the water on its lizard-like legs, sucking up fish, worms, insect larvae, and crustaceans in its wide, smiling mouth. But what makes the axolotl really remarkable is that, unlike other salamanders and almost all other amphibians, it very rarely develops into its final land-living stage.

When it hatches, an axolotl has gills rising in feathered pairs from either side of its head and a little fin that runs the length of its body. It also has very basic lungs, which allow it to gulp air from the surface. But while most other amphibians go on to lose their tail and gills and develop their lungs, the axolotl keeps its larval form all its life. Like a tadpole that never grows up, it can never leave the water.

In the past, this gave the axolotl an advantage. By not putting its energy into transforming its body, the axolotl is able to reproduce sooner. From six to twelve months of age, axolotls are ready to breed, searching for mates in the murky water. They can breed several times a year, and lay many eggs. For 10,000 years, this has ensured their survival in Mexico's lakes and waterways.

Today, however, the axolotl is racing toward extinction in the wild. All that remains of its habitat are about 65 square miles (170 square kilometers) of canals, highly polluted and teeming with predators such as carp and tilapia, which were introduced by humans just fifty years ago. Axolotls thrive elsewhere in the world only as pets or in laboratories, where scientists seek to unlock their secrets.

Axolotls have long been seen as almost mythical creatures. They are named for Xolotl, a dog-headed god from Aztec mythology who is said to have to transformed himself into an axolotl to escape being sacrificed. And scientists have discovered that axolotls really do have amazing powers: they are able to regrow missing limbs without any scarring and can rebuild their jaws, spine, and even parts of their brain.

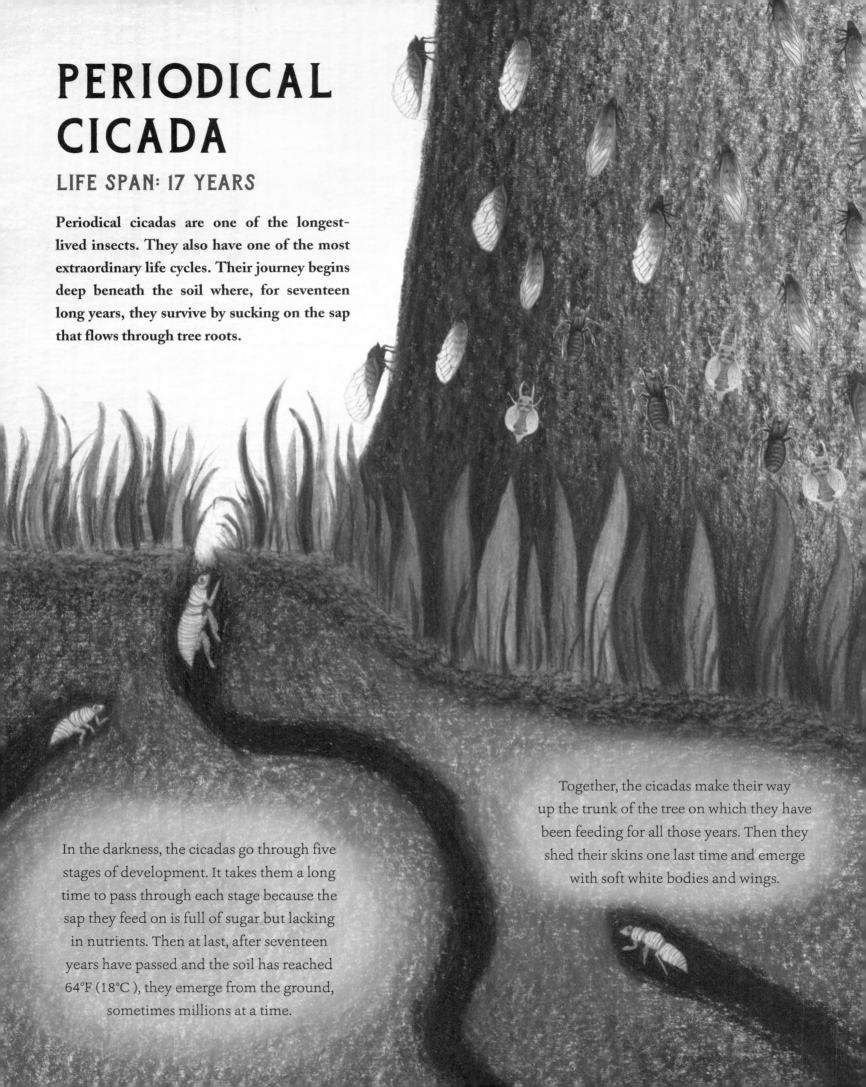

PERIODICAL CICADA

LIFE SPAN: 17 YEARS

Periodical cicadas are one of the longest-lived insects. They also have one of the most extraordinary life cycles. Their journey begins deep beneath the soil where, for seventeen long years, they survive by sucking on the sap that flows through tree roots.

In the darkness, the cicadas go through five stages of development. It takes them a long time to pass through each stage because the sap they feed on is full of sugar but lacking in nutrients. Then at last, after seventeen years have passed and the soil has reached 64°F (18°C), they emerge from the ground, sometimes millions at a time.

Together, the cicadas make their way up the trunk of the tree on which they have been feeding for all those years. Then they shed their skins one last time and emerge with soft white bodies and wings.

The cicadas wait for their bodies to harden, turning a dark, earthy brown. They now have bright-red eyes and transparent orange-flecked wings. Then the males begin to sing, making a strange reverberating sound that fills the air. The females respond by flicking their wings: *click! click! click!*

After mating, the females lay their eggs using a special tube, called an ovipositor, on the tip of the abdomen. This ovipositor is sharp and pointed, and the females use them like swords, slicing into the tree to lay their eggs.

As adults, cicadas only live five to six weeks. They disappear almost as quickly as they came, leaving only their eggs and their larval skins behind. Why the strange life cycle? Scientists think it could be that by emerging after such a long time underground, they escape the life cycle of their would-be predators. And how can the cicadas tell when seventeen years have passed? Nobody knows. It is one of nature's mysteries.

TRAPDOOR SPIDER

FEMALE LIFE SPAN: 20 TO 40 YEARS
MALE LIFE SPAN: 5 TO 7 YEARS

How long does a spider live for? For a common house spider, only a few years. For a tarantula, possibly twenty years or more. But the oldest known spider, an armored trapdoor spider, was an astonishing forty-three years old when she died. She spent her entire life in one tiny patch of southwest Australia, beneath the branches of an acacia tree.

Trapdoor spiders are born in their mother's silk-lined burrow. The baby spiderlings live there for six months, until the arrival of the autumn rains. The mother then unseals the burrow to release the spiderlings into the world.

A young trapdoor spider builds a burrow by making a circle in the earth that is just a fraction larger than its body and then digs down into the soil. The burrow is lined with silk to make a small underground shelter. A silken door is woven across the entrance and attached on one side so it can open and close. Next, the spider collects twigs to arrange in a spiral pattern around the doorway.

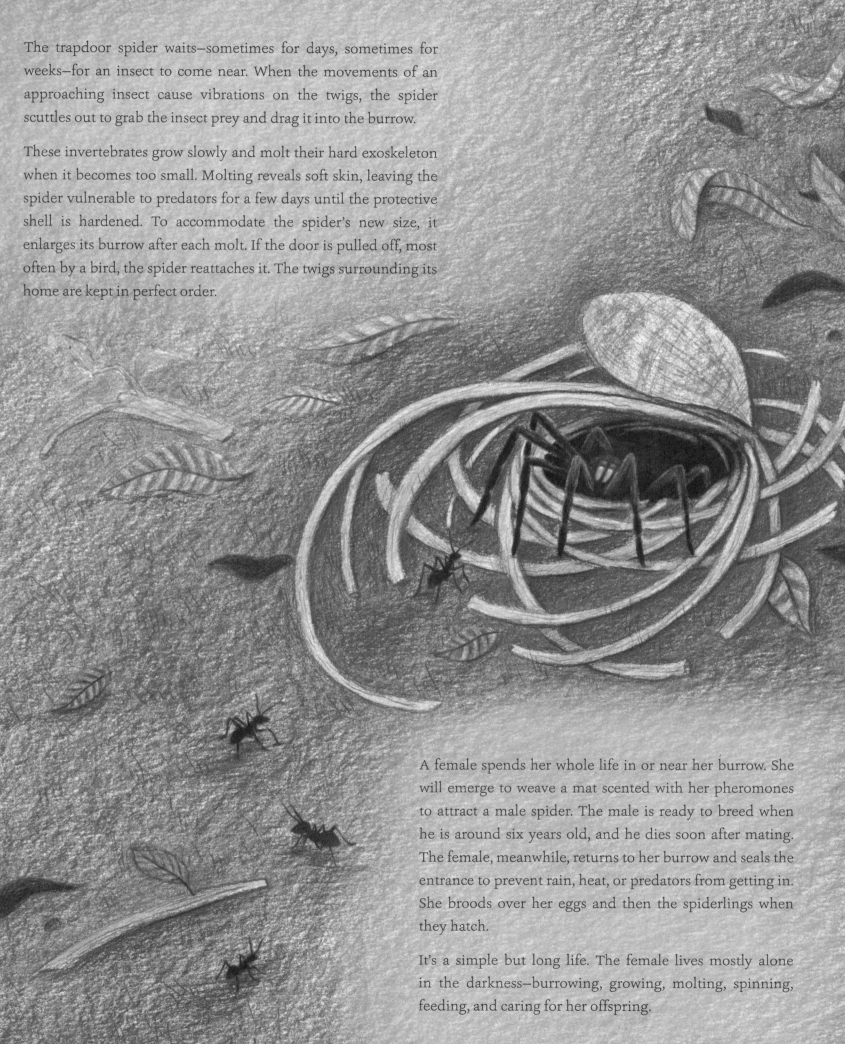

The trapdoor spider waits—sometimes for days, sometimes for weeks—for an insect to come near. When the movements of an approaching insect cause vibrations on the twigs, the spider scuttles out to grab the insect prey and drag it into the burrow.

These invertebrates grow slowly and molt their hard exoskeleton when it becomes too small. Molting reveals soft skin, leaving the spider vulnerable to predators for a few days until the protective shell is hardened. To accommodate the spider's new size, it enlarges its burrow after each molt. If the door is pulled off, most often by a bird, the spider reattaches it. The twigs surrounding its home are kept in perfect order.

A female spends her whole life in or near her burrow. She will emerge to weave a mat scented with her pheromones to attract a male spider. The male is ready to breed when he is around six years old, and he dies soon after mating. The female, meanwhile, returns to her burrow and seals the entrance to prevent rain, heat, or predators from getting in. She broods over her eggs and then the spiderlings when they hatch.

It's a simple but long life. The female lives mostly alone in the darkness—burrowing, growing, molting, spinning, feeding, and caring for her offspring.

GRIZZLY BEAR

LIFE SPAN: 20 TO 30 YEARS

It is October and winter is coming, but the female grizzly bear is ready. She has a den—a cozy hole lined with grass, leaves, and moss. All summer she feasted as much as she could to put on enough fat to last her through the winter. She gorged on salmon from the river, and then, when autumn rolled in, she searched for seeds, nuts, and berries. Now, as the temperature drops, she settles down to sleep. Her body temperature falls from 100°F (38°C) to 91°F (33°C). Her heart rate slows to below a quarter of its normal rate. Her sleep is not as deep as hibernating animals—she can wake at the slightest disturbance, ready to defend herself in case of attack—but left undisturbed, she will sleep for four to seven months.

Amazingly, pregnant females even give birth during their winter rest. The cubs, born tiny, blind, and hairless, will suckle from their mother as she sleeps, warming themselves in the thick fur of her belly.

When a female grizzly bear finally rouses in the spring, she will have lost a third of her body weight. By then, her cubs are ready to face the world. They have grown strong on their mother's milk and have thick fur coats of their own. Their mother will take them out into the world, teaching them how to hunt and what to eat, and they will stay with her for up to four years.

Grizzly bears spend between a third and half of their lives asleep. Their long winter rest is a strategy for survival, as there is little food in the winter months. And it is a strategy that works. Animals that spend winter in a deep sleep tend to have longer lives than animals that don't, as they are much less likely to die during winter. It works not just for individuals, but also for the species: grizzly bears have been sleeping through icy winters now for more than a million years.

BRANDT'S BAT

LIFE SPAN: 40 YEARS

Bats are a hugely successful animal group, making up a fifth of all known mammal species. They are the only mammals that can truly fly, on wings made of thin skin stretched between their elongated fingers. Most are nocturnal, and to help them navigate in the dark and track down prey, they use echolocation: sending out sounds and then listening to the returning echo.

When it comes to life spans, bats break all the rules. Most mammals with small body sizes live shorter lives (see page 19), but scientists have found twenty-two bat species that live for more than twenty years, and five bat species that live for more than thirty years in the wild. The insect-eating Brandt's bat weighs just a fraction of an ounce but lives for around forty years—giving it a longer life span than any other mammal for its body size. One Brandt's bat, captured in Siberia in 2005, was forty-one years old, and showed no signs of aging. So how do bats manage to live such long and healthy lives?

It is partly due to the power of flight. Most flying animals, including birds, live longer than non-flying animals of a similar size, as being able to fly means they are able to escape from predators more easily. Bats also live together in flocks, which makes them less likely to be picked off by predators. Vampire bats, one of the longest-lived bat species, will also keep one another from starving. Female vampire bats have been recorded sharing blood from meals.

Most long-lived bat species hibernate. They are able to lower their body temperature and sleep through long winters, enabling them to survive when there is less food to be had, often in the safety of caves. In Siberia, the Brandt's bat has one of the longest hibernation periods, from late September to the middle of June, giving it just three months of activity each year.

Scientists are now studying the genes of bats to see how their DNA helps them to live for so long. If humans lived as long as bats, adjusted for size, we could live for up to 240 years. It could well be that bats hold the answers to humanity's search for longer and healthier lives.

ECHIDNA

LIFE SPAN: 45 YEARS

Echidnas are one of the world's oldest living mammals. They have been around for millions of years, surviving even the mass extinction that wiped out the dinosaurs. Today, along with duck-billed platypuses, they are the only living members of an ancient group of egg-laying mammals, called monotremes, that once dominated Australia. There are just four species: the short-beaked echidna, still found in Australia, and three species of long-beaked echidna, all endangered, found only in the hilly forests of Papua New Guinea.

Adult echidnas are covered in prickles. They have short, stubby legs and long, fleshy noses, which they use to pick up electrical signals from their insect prey. Among their many curious habits are the "love trains" that males form at the beginning of the breeding season. During the winter months, up to eleven male echidnas can be seen lining up nose to tail behind a female, all hoping to become her mate.

Around two weeks after mating, a female echidna lays a soft, leathery egg, which she places in a pouch on her stomach. After hatching, a baby echidna, known as a puggle, is no bigger than a jelly bean. With tiny claws, its clings onto its mother's pouch hair, lapping at milk that she secretes through glands at the front of the pouch.

A puggle stays in its mother's pouch for around seven weeks, until its prickles begin to emerge. The mother then places her spiky baby in a burrow, returning to it every five to ten days to give it milk and food. At around seven months, it is ready to make its own way in the world.

Averaging 90°F (32°C), echidnas have the lowest active body temperature of all mammals except the platypus. Scientists think this, coupled with their slow metabolism, is the key to echidnas' long lives. They have been reported to survive for up to forty-five years in the wild.

Echidnas also have the ability to lower their body temperature further still, which puts them into a state known as torpor, in which they barely eat or move for days at a time. This helps them to survive when their habitat is struck by bushfire, which frequently happens. By hiding in an underground burrow or inside fallen logs, they can be protected from the raging flames and can stay there afterward, when food is scarce.

What we know of echidnas makes them both puzzling and fascinating. These elusive and ancient creatures have only recently been studied in the wild, so we are just beginning to unravel their mysteries.

ORANGUTAN

LIFE SPAN: 45 YEARS

Orangutans are great apes and one of our closest relatives. The name means "person of the forest," and they are found in the rain forests of Borneo and Sumatra. There, they live long, slow lives high among the treetops.

An orangutan moves by clambering from branch to branch, cautiously climbing, rarely jumping. Each day is spent mostly eating, or simply at rest. In the evening, an orangutan will build a treetop nest out of leafy branches, usually in a different place each night.

Sumatran orangutans are the slowest to grow and breed of any land mammal. A mother will give birth to her first baby at around fifteen years old and will have just one baby at a time.

For the first four to five years of its life, a baby Sumatran orangutan clings to its mother's fur as she moves through the forest, until it has the strength and agility to clamber about on its own. A baby will then stay with its mother until it is eight years old, suckling on her milk and learning the ways of the forest. The bond between them is incredibly strong.

This long childhood—the longest in the animal kingdom apart from humans—is vital for an orangutan's survival. These intelligent creatures have so much to learn, from the fruits they can eat to nest-building to how to collect termites or make a leaf-umbrella in the rain. Only when a young orangutan is ready to survive on its own will its mother breed again.

And it is this long childhood that also makes orangutans so vulnerable. They are losing their habitat, fast, as their rain forest homes are chopped down. A population, once lost, is very slow to recover. Each female will only have, at most, four to five babies in her lifetime. Despite the leisurely pace of their lives, time is running out for the last great ape of Asia.

LAYSAN ALBATROSS

LIFE SPAN: 50 YEARS

On a tiny speck of an island in the middle of the North Pacific Ocean, more than 1,900 miles (3,000 kilometers) from the Midway Atoll, a female Laysan albatross named Wisdom comes in to land. She is around seventy years old (the world's oldest known wild bird), and she has come to meet her mate.

Laysan albatrosses are one of the longest-lived birds. They spend most of their lives at sea, typically gathering on remote, far-flung islands, in order to breed. With wingspans of nearly 7 feet (2 meters), they soar over the open ocean, riding the wind and using their wide wings to glide for hours without rest.

But once every year or two, an albatross leaves its ocean life to begin the arduous task of raising a chick. An albatross will always return to the same nest site, in the hope of meeting its mate from previous years. For Wisdom, this is a male named Akeakamai. When they meet, they court each other to reaffirm the bonds that can last a lifetime. They touch bills, then mirror each other's movements: bobbing their heads, placing their bill under a wing. Then they sit together, preening each other and snuggling up close. Only then is it time to mate.

A female Laysan albatross lays just one egg, because the parents can only care for one chick at a time. They take turns sitting on the egg and going out to sea to hunt for food. After two months, the egg is ready to hatch, and the parents will need to care for the chick for five more months. With luck, the fledgling will then successfully take to the skies to spend its first three years at sea without ever touching land.

Each egg is vitally important to the survival of the species. Albatrosses face many threats: rising sea levels, temperature changes, increasing storms, death from fishing equipment and plastic. Mammals such as mice and rats, introduced by humans onto their nesting islands, feast on their eggs and chicks. The numbers of these feathered giants are now falling fast. Hope lies in grand matriarchs like Wisdom, returning year after to year to raise the next generation.

Once the chick has fledged, adult albatrosses return to the ocean, swooping over the sea's surface in search of food, including fish, octopus, cuttlefish, and squid. They can travel almost 500 miles (800 kilometers) a day on their wide wings, at speeds of 50 miles (80 kilometers) per hour.

KĀKĀPŌ

LIFE SPAN: 60 TO 100 YEARS

Solitary, fat, and flightless, the kākāpō, a parrot from New Zealand, is one of the longest-lived birds on earth.

Kākāpōs come out at night, waddling across the forest floor in search of fruit and nuts. Having opted for life on the ground, they have no need to stay light. Instead, their bones are filled with marrow and they can store large amounts of body fat. Despite appearances, they are expert tree climbers, and their stubby wings help them flap their way back down to the ground.

Everything about a kākāpō's life moves slowly. They do not run from danger, but instead stand very still, relying on the moss-like camouflage of their feathers to remain undetected. Males do not start breeding until they are four years old, females at six, and they breed more slowly than any other bird. Mating only takes place every two to four years or so, when the rimu tree, and other conifers like the rimu, produce a bumper crop of fruit, providing the kākāpōs with the vital vitamins they need in order to reproduce.

The unhurried nature of the kākāpōs extends to the males' courtship. During the breeding season, a male will walk 3 miles (5 kilometers) to a special area, known as a lek, to compete for female attention. Each male digs a shallow bowl in the ground, then spends up to eight hours a night making loud booming calls. This can last for up to four months. If a female is interested, she approaches the bowl along tracks the male has cleared.

But all the features that make kākāpōs so unusual and charming are now their downfall. They evolved in a different world, free of mammals, where their only predators were the eagles that would swoop down from the treetops. The kākāpōs' camouflage used to protect them. But the arrival of Europeans to New Zealand brought rodents, cats, and other mammals, and kākāpō numbers plummeted.

By the 1970s, it was thought only a few males remained. Then scientists discovered a tiny population of breeding kākāpōs. They were taken to small, predator-free islands and cared for under an intensive breeding program. Today, there are just over two hundred of these friendly birds left, slowly clawing their way back from the brink of extinction.

AFRICAN ELEPHANT

LIFE SPAN: 60 TO 70 YEARS

An old female elephant stands on the savanna, gazing across the dusty landscape. It has not rained for many months and the herd is thirsty. Should they stay where they are, and hope that the rains will come? Or travel under the hot sun, searching for water?

Like most elephant herds, this one is led by the oldest and most experienced female—the matriarch—and it will be her decision. This herd is lucky. Their matriarch knows just what to do. She can remember exactly where to find water in times of drought, and the best place for fruit and grasses.

Elephants have long lives—one of the longest of any land mammal—and long memories. A herd's survival depends on the knowledge and experience of their elders. The young learn from the old. Their longevity means they do not have to rush through life. The slow, unhurried pace begins with a pregnancy that lasts twenty-two months, the longest of any mammal.

At around fourteen years old, a male elephant joins a group of bull elephants, known as a bachelor herd. In this herd, he will discover how to find out if a female is fertile, how to fight, and where to roam. Around ten years later, a male will begin a life on his own. Females, however, stay with their herd all their lives. They learn from their sisters, mothers, aunts, and cousins how to raise a calf of their own. They will share in the care of other calves, babysitting, caretaking, and protecting them from predators. The wise old grandmothers carry with them a treasure trove of information, as crucial to the herds' survival as each newborn calf.

SALTWATER CROCODILE

LIFE SPAN: 70 YEARS

There's something startlingly prehistoric about a saltwater crocodile. And that's not surprising. They come from an ancient line of crocodilians dating back over 200 million years and still look very similar to some of their armor-plated ancestors.

Today, the saltwater crocodile is the largest of its kind, and the largest reptile on earth. It is also the longest-lived of any crocodile species, reaching seventy years or more. Salties, as they are known, are survivors: tough, robust, and super predators.

Large adults can stay underwater for at least an hour, reducing their heart rates to two to three beats per minute. Camouflaged, with only their eyes and the tips of their noses above the surface, they remain motionless until prey comes close. Then they lunge with terrifying speed, grabbing their prey with one of the most powerful bites of any animal. They are also able to survive terrible injuries, such as a lost tail, jaw, or limb.

But the key to their success as a species, and their ability to live for so long, comes from their cold-bloodedness. This means that crocodiles don't control their body temperature in the way that mammals do. Instead, to maintain an ideal temperature, they move back and forth between warm and cool parts of their environment. This uses less energy, which means they need less food. Crocodiles can survive for over a year without eating.

There is much more, however, to a saltwater crocodile than being a "cold-blooded killer." They are intelligent and able to adapt quickly to changes in their environment. They also make caring, attentive mothers. Females build nests out of mounds of mud and vegetation, so their eggs are kept safe and dry, and guard them closely.

When the baby crocodiles are ready to hatch, they call out to their mother. She uncovers the nest and carefully carries the hatchlings to the water in her mouth, up to fifteen at a time. There she watches over them until they have learned to swim.

Only 1 percent of baby crocodiles make it to adulthood. Most falling victim to fish, snakes, and birds of prey. And it takes a long time for a saltwater crocodile to reach breeding age: ten to twelve years for females, and sixteen for males. But once a saltwater crocodile is fully grown, no animal, other than humans, can harm them.

AMERICAN LOBSTER

LIFE SPAN: 100+ YEARS

Throughout our lives, the millions of cells that make up our bodies are constantly replacing themselves at a rate of millions every second. But as we age, our cells stop being able to copy themselves. This leads to aging, a process known as senescence. We grow weaker. We are no longer able to reproduce, and our metabolism slows.

Lobsters, however, can keep repairing and renewing their cells for much longer than most other animals. Adult lobsters can even regrow any limbs lost by accident or during a fight, and lobsters keep growing and reproducing right up until the end of their lives. In fact, the older a female lobster, the more babies she is able to have, as larger females can carry more eggs. Older, larger lobsters that are able to travel further out to release their eggs have more offspring, as they are able to avoid damaging pollution and any sediment that might smother the eggs.

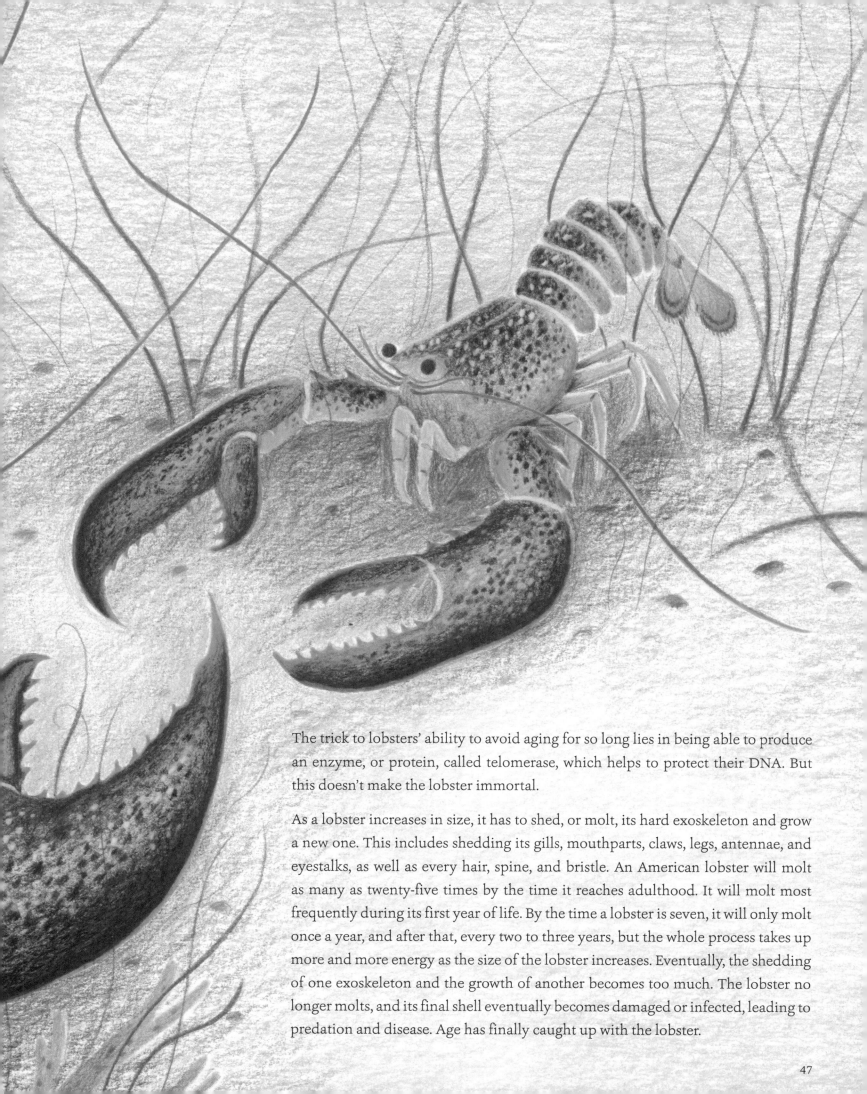

The trick to lobsters' ability to avoid aging for so long lies in being able to produce an enzyme, or protein, called telomerase, which helps to protect their DNA. But this doesn't make the lobster immortal.

As a lobster increases in size, it has to shed, or molt, its hard exoskeleton and grow a new one. This includes shedding its gills, mouthparts, claws, legs, antennae, and eyestalks, as well as every hair, spine, and bristle. An American lobster will molt as many as twenty-five times by the time it reaches adulthood. It will molt most frequently during its first year of life. By the time a lobster is seven, it will only molt once a year, and after that, every two to three years, but the whole process takes up more and more energy as the size of the lobster increases. Eventually, the shedding of one exoskeleton and the growth of another becomes too much. The lobster no longer molts, and its final shell eventually becomes damaged or infected, leading to predation and disease. Age has finally caught up with the lobster.

ORANGE ROUGHY

LIFE SPAN: 100+ YEARS

Travel east from the coast of New Zealand and then down beneath the waves: deep, deep down, and deeper still, into the sunless depths. The water grows dark and cold. Life here is slow, almost as if time itself has been suspended. There are trails carved by drifting icebergs, still visible after 18,000 years. There are mountains, known as seamounts, that rise up from the seafloor.

It is down here that the orange roughy lives—one of the longest-lived fish in the ocean. Some individuals have been here for over a century, others longer still. One specimen studied by scientists in New Zealand was estimated to have been between 230 and 245 years old. This fish was born in the late 1700s and lived through the French Revolution, the American Civil War, and two World Wars before it was plucked from the ocean depths.

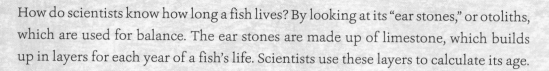

How do scientists know how long a fish lives? By looking at its "ear stones," or otoliths, which are used for balance. The ear stones are made up of limestone, which builds up in layers for each year of a fish's life. Scientists use these layers to calculate its age.

Orange roughy feed on small fish and crustaceans carried by the ocean currents. But despite being predators, they are sluggish creatures, and when there is no food to eat, they become slower still, barely moving for long periods at a time.

They take at least twenty years to mature, grow very slowly, and do not breed every year. It is this slow-paced life that has made them so vulnerable to overfishing. It was once thought that orange roughy only lived for thirty years, and it was presumed they would cope with being fished in huge numbers, with their populations recovering quickly. Instead, their numbers crashed. Even in places where fishing for orange roughy has been restricted, it will take fifty years or more for the population of these remarkably long-lived fish to recover.

GALÁPAGOS GIANT TORTOISE
LIFE SPAN: 100+ YEARS

About 620 miles (1,000 kilometers) off the coast of Ecuador lie the Galápagos Islands. Here, amid rocks and cacti and pounding waves, roam giant tortoises, the largest of all tortoise species. They live for more than a hundred years and are found nowhere else on earth.

But how did they get there? Scientists think that between two to three million years ago, some giant tortoises drifted out to sea, either by themselves or on mats of vegetation, until they came to land on these far-flung islands.

For two to three million years, the giant tortoises lived slow, peaceful lives in isolation. There were no predators for adult tortoises to fear, and no prey to catch. They spent their time munching on cacti, grasses, and fruit. In the cooler months, they would sleep in the morning and the afternoon, only stirring into action around midday. In the hot season, they sought shade from the fierce midday sun or cooled off by wallowing in muddy pools. When food and water were scarce, they slept, often for weeks at a time. The environment was tough, but the tortoises were perfectly adapted to it, able to last up to a year without food or water.

But then, in the nineteenth century, sailors discovered the tortoises were an excellent source of fresh meat, and so they kept them on board their ships. The tortoises' ability to survive long periods without food or water now was now being used against them. By 1959, most of the giant tortoise populations on each island were endangered or on the brink of extinction.

One of those was the Pinta Island tortoise. In 1971, there was just one of its kind left, a male known as Lonesome George. Scientists searched his island, desperately hoping to find him a mate to save the species—but with no success. Lonesome George lived in captivity for another forty years, gaining worldwide fame, but had no offspring.

But there is still hope for other Galápagos tortoise species. In February 2019, a female Fernandina tortoise, a species not seen for 110 years, was found alive and well on her lava-flooded island. She was taken to a breeding center and the hunt is now on to find her a mate. Scientists are hopeful, having found tracks and feces that they believe belong to another Fernandina tortoise. With time and science on their side, there's hope for these giant tortoises yet.

BOWHEAD WHALE

LIFE SPAN: 200+ YEARS

In 2007, newspaper headlines announced an amazing discovery: a bowhead whale had been found off the coast of Alaska, with a 130-year-old harpoon lodged in her shoulder. The arrow fragment, a leftover from a failed hunt, was dated to around 1880, suggesting that the whale had been swimming through Arctic waters since Victorian times. Here was evidence that bowhead whales are the oldest-living mammals on earth. As the Inuit have long said, these whales live at least two human lifetimes.

Further research, published in 2019, revealed something even more incredible: the average life span of a bowhead whale is 268 years. This was determined using a genetic "clock," which is when scientists study a life-form's genes to predict how long it can live.

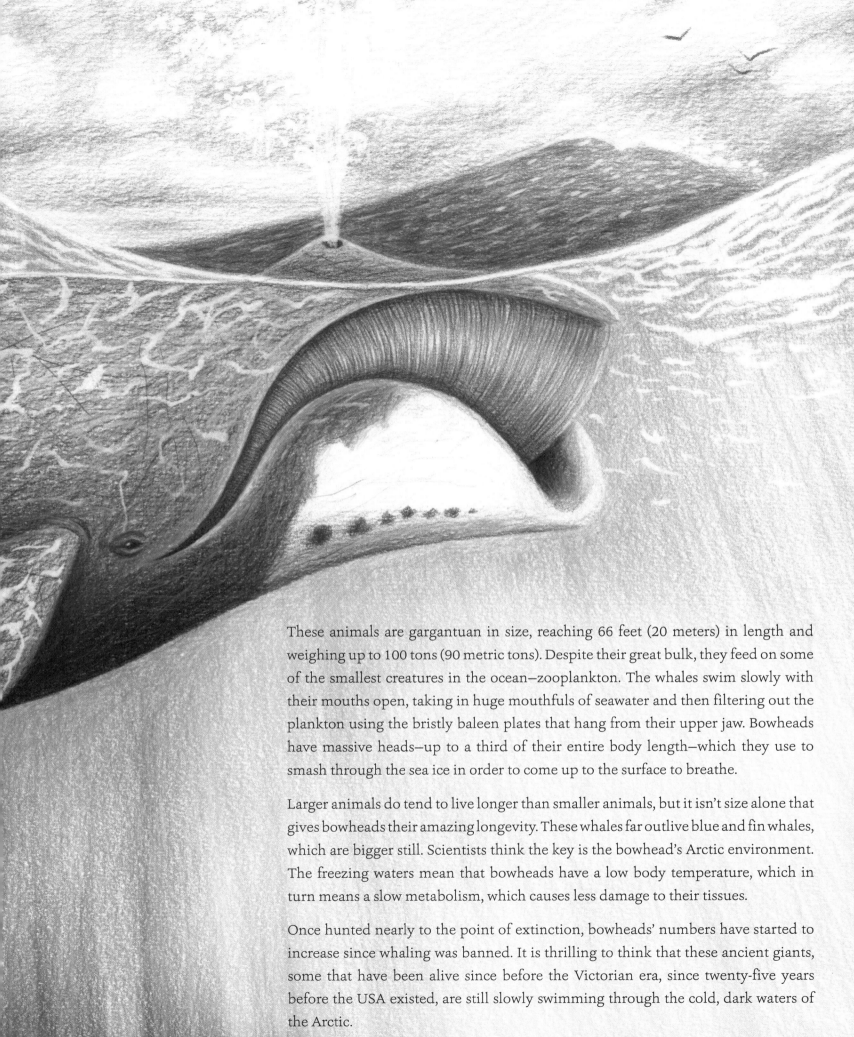

These animals are gargantuan in size, reaching 66 feet (20 meters) in length and weighing up to 100 tons (90 metric tons). Despite their great bulk, they feed on some of the smallest creatures in the ocean—zooplankton. The whales swim slowly with their mouths open, taking in huge mouthfuls of seawater and then filtering out the plankton using the bristly baleen plates that hang from their upper jaw. Bowheads have massive heads—up to a third of their entire body length—which they use to smash through the sea ice in order to come up to the surface to breathe.

Larger animals do tend to live longer than smaller animals, but it isn't size alone that gives bowheads their amazing longevity. These whales far outlive blue and fin whales, which are bigger still. Scientists think the key is the bowhead's Arctic environment. The freezing waters mean that bowheads have a low body temperature, which in turn means a slow metabolism, which causes less damage to their tissues.

Once hunted nearly to the point of extinction, bowheads' numbers have started to increase since whaling was banned. It is thrilling to think that these ancient giants, some that have been alive since before the Victorian era, since twenty-five years before the USA existed, are still slowly swimming through the cold, dark waters of the Arctic.

GREENLAND SHARK

LIFE SPAN: UP TO 400 YEARS

Greenland sharks are not immediately appealing. They are huge—about the length of a large car—with squat-shaped bodies, stunted fins, toxic skin, blunt snouts, and gaping mouths. Many have wormlike parasites dangling from the fronts of their eyes.

They can be found swimming stealthily through the cold waters of the North Atlantic and the Arctic, from depths of around 7,200 feet (2,200 meters) to the icy surface, where they have been known to sneak up on sleeping seals. At other times, they scavenge whatever they can find, dead or alive—they're not fussy. Individuals have been discovered with the remains of polar bears, reindeer, and even horses in their digestive systems.

Aside from their bizarre eating habits, very little else is known about Greenland sharks. The deep, dark freezing waters they favor are so inhospitable to humans that the first video of a live shark was only recorded in 2003.

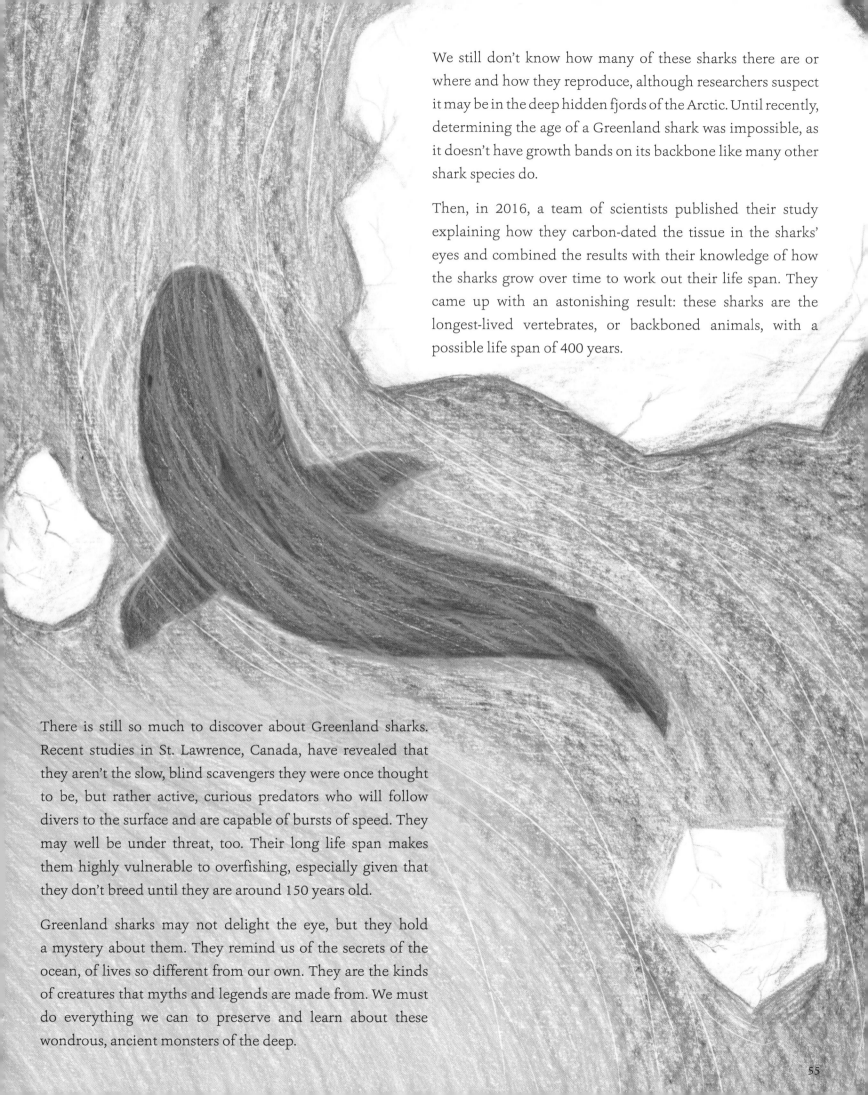

We still don't know how many of these sharks there are or where and how they reproduce, although researchers suspect it may be in the deep hidden fjords of the Arctic. Until recently, determining the age of a Greenland shark was impossible, as it doesn't have growth bands on its backbone like many other shark species do.

Then, in 2016, a team of scientists published their study explaining how they carbon-dated the tissue in the sharks' eyes and combined the results with their knowledge of how the sharks grow over time to work out their life span. They came up with an astonishing result: these sharks are the longest-lived vertebrates, or backboned animals, with a possible life span of 400 years.

There is still so much to discover about Greenland sharks. Recent studies in St. Lawrence, Canada, have revealed that they aren't the slow, blind scavengers they were once thought to be, but rather active, curious predators who will follow divers to the surface and are capable of bursts of speed. They may well be under threat, too. Their long life span makes them highly vulnerable to overfishing, especially given that they don't breed until they are around 150 years old.

Greenland sharks may not delight the eye, but they hold a mystery about them. They remind us of the secrets of the ocean, of lives so different from our own. They are the kinds of creatures that myths and legends are made from. We must do everything we can to preserve and learn about these wondrous, ancient monsters of the deep.

OCEAN QUAHOG

LIFE SPAN: 400 YEARS

The ocean quahog, a type of clam, doesn't look like much. A tiny, soft-bodied animal with a hinged shell, that can fit in the palm of your hand. But this clam has a secret superpower.

It lives an unassuming life, buried in the seabed of the North Atlantic, filtering out food from the water with a long, tubelike structure known as a siphon. Sometimes the siphon is all you can see above the seabed, and every so often its end is nibbled off by hungry fish.

Every year, these quahogs release sperm and eggs into the water, which are then fertilized. The larvae drift in the water for thirty days until they develop into juveniles and settle to the bottom. There they begin to grow, very, very slowly.

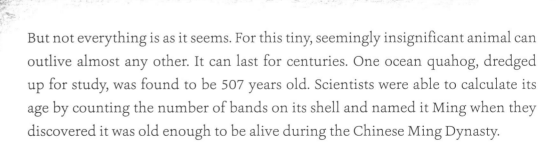

But not everything is as it seems. For this tiny, seemingly insignificant animal can outlive almost any other. It can last for centuries. One ocean quahog, dredged up for study, was found to be 507 years old. Scientists were able to calculate its age by counting the number of bands on its shell and named it Ming when they discovered it was old enough to be alive during the Chinese Ming Dynasty.

Just as amazingly, these tiny creatures can also reveal the secrets of our past. By looking at the quahogs' shells, scientists can study changes in the ocean over the centuries, from how warm the seas were to how salty, and begin to understand what were once the natural rhythms of our climate, now masked by human activity. These ancient treasures are more than just mollusks. They are a window into another world.

GLASS SPONGE

LIFE SPAN: 11,000 YEARS

There are a few animals, all found in the deep sea, that can live even longer than the quahog. One of those is the deep-sea sponge, which may also have been one of the very first multicellular animals (organisms made of more than one cell) on earth, first evolving more than 650 million years ago.

Individual sponges can live for thousands of years. One particular sponge, *Monorhaphis chuni*, found in the East China Sea, was estimated to be 11,000 years old. A type of glass sponge, it has a skeleton made of silica—a mineral used in glass. It can grow to nearly 10 feet (3 meters) tall, with a single long, spectacular spine, called a spicule. This spicule is just one centimeter thick and anchors the sponge to the seafloor.

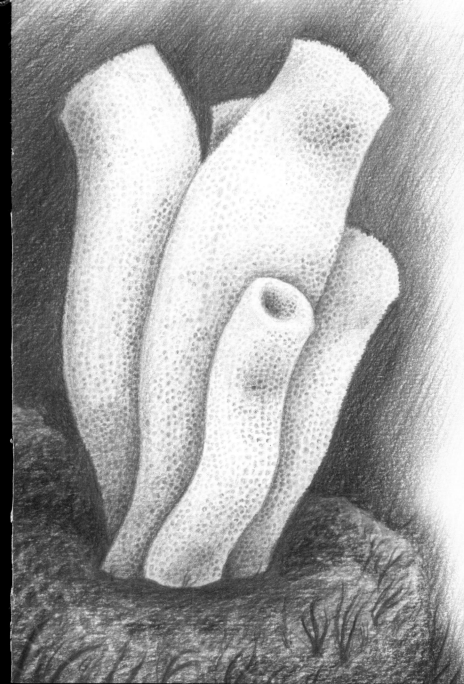

What is it about the deep sea that makes it home to so many long-lived creatures? At great depths, animals are protected from temperature changes and violent storms. These stable environments go hand in hand with longevity. Animals in shallower waters are also at greater risk of predation, so they are less likely to evolve to be able to repair their bodies and achieve a healthy old age.

For deep-sea sponges that spend their lives fixed in one place, there is another advantage: sponges can break off into two or more individuals, each of which can regenerate into a new (but genetically identical) sponge. While many parts may die off, an individual will always be made up of some young pieces, which constantly replace the older ones.

It is an exciting time for deep-sea discoveries. Scientists are just beginning to find more of these long-lived species. At the same time, they are starting to work out what secrets these life-forms can reveal about the distant past.

IMMORTAL JELLYFISH
LIFE SPAN: IMMORTAL

It's incredible to think of animals living for hundreds of years, like the Greenland shark in the freezing waters of the Arctic, or a thousand-year-old glass sponge, deep down at the bottom of the ocean. But it is even more amazing to imagine an animal that reaches the end of its life, only to begin all over again. In the late 1980s, scientists discovered that a tiny jellyfish, no bigger than our little fingernail, could do just that.

Turritopsis dohrnii, otherwise known as the immortal jellyfish, begins its life as a larva, a tiny creature that swims through the water looking for something—a rock, a boat's hull—to attach itself to. There it develops into a tube-shaped polyp with branching stalks that end in little buds. It stays there for a while, growing into a colony of polyps. Then the buds at the ends of its stalks begin to swell, before sprouting into tiny baby jellyfish with bell-shaped domes and dangling tentacles.

For most jellyfish, this stage—known as the medusa stage—is the final phase of its life. The medusa produces eggs or sperm, and then dies. But not the immortal jellyfish . . .

At any sign of threat, from starvation to physical danger, the jellyfish can transform itself back into a polyp for its life cycle to begin again. This would be like if a butterfly transformed back into a caterpillar, or a frog turned into a tadpole. The immortal jellyfish can do this again, and again, and again.

The immortal jellyfish, then, has escaped death. Although perhaps its immortality comes at a high price. It is, after all, a very simple creature, with no heart, no brain, and just one opening for feeding and waste.

Some would argue that the jellyfish isn't truly immortal. It can still die by being eaten or from disease. Moreover, the cells that make up the new jellyfish are not the same as the old one. They have been changed in the regeneration process, so that the new jellyfish is a copy, a clone, rather than the exact same organism.

But something truly, breathtakingly remarkable is still happening here. Instead of death, this jellyfish becomes young again, in an endless cycle. It is one of the most rule-breaking discoveries of our time.

HOW LONG ANIMALS LIVE

Our planet is around 4.5 billion years old. Even though an animal's time on earth, by comparison, is fleeting, it is still startlingly different from one species to the next. Some animals live much shorter lives than us, others outlive us by far. This illustration captures both the variety of time on earth, as well as the amazing diversity of life with which we share our planet.

1. Adult mayfly: 5 minutes–24 hours
2. Honeybee: 5–7 weeks
3. Monarch butterfly: 2 weeks–8 months
4. Pygmy goby: 59 days
5. Labord's chameleon: 4–5 months
6. Opossum: 1–2 years
7. Etruscan shrew: 1 year–2 years
8. Giant Pacific octopus: 3–5 years
9. Male trapdoor spider: 5–7 years
10. Axolotl: 10–15 years
11. Cicada: 17 years
12. Female trapdoor spider: 20–40 years
13. Grizzly bear: 20–30 years
14. Brandt's bat: 40 years
15. Echidna: 45 years
16. Orangutan: 45 years
17. Laysan albatross: 50 years
18. Kākāpō: 60–100 years
19. African elephant: 60–70 years
20. Saltwater crocodile: 70 years
21. American lobster: 100+ years
22. Orange roughy: 100+ years
23. Galápagos giant tortoise: 100+ years
24. Bowhead whale: 200+ years
25. Greenland shark: 400 years
26. Ocean quahog: 400 years
27. Glass sponge: 11,000 years
28. Immortal jellyfish: immortal

ABOUT THE ILLUSTRATOR

Jesse Hodgson studied illustration at the University of the West of England. She now lives and works in Bristol, England, where she has a studio space. She is the author and illustrator of several picture books. Her illustrations for *Pongo* were Highly Commended for the 2012 Macmillan Prize for Illustration.

ABOUT THE AUTHOR

Lily Murray grew up in the wilds of snowy nowhere, spending much of her time talking to animals and making up stories. She has continued to do this in her adult life, and now writes both fiction and nonfiction books for children. Her titles include big books about dinosaurs, rhyming books about dinosaurs, and stories about escaped hot dogs.